RIBBONS, LACE, AND MOMENTS OF GRACE

Inspiration for the Mother of the Bride

By

LEIGH ANN THOMAS

RIBBONS, LACE, AND MOMENTS OF GRACE BY LEIGH ANN
THOMAS
Published by SonRise Devotionals, an imprint of
Lighthouse Publishing of the Carolinas
2333 Barton Oaks Dr., Raleigh, NC, 27614

ISBN: 978-1-946016-15-7
Copyright © 2017 by Leigh Ann Thomas
Cover design by Elaina Lee
Interior design by Atritex, www.atritex.com

Available in print from your local bookstore, online, or from the
publisher at: www.lpcbooks.com

For more information on this book and the author,
visit: www.leighathomas.com

Brought to you by the creative team at Lighthouse Publishing of the
Carolinas: Eddie Jones, Shonda Savage, Denise Loock, and Cindy
Sproles.

Library of Congress Cataloging-in-Publication Data
Thomas, Leigh Ann
Ribbons, Lace, and Moments of Grace / Leigh Ann Thomas 1st ed.

For my mom,
who set the standard for sacrificial loving and giving

She is clothed with strength and dignity.
Proverbs 31:25

Praise for *Ribbons, Lace, and Moments of Grace*

A wedding can be a hectic time—for the bride *and* for the mother of the bride. Even moms who have traveled this road before need time to reflect, renew, and rejoice. *Ribbons, Lace, and Moments of Grace* provides just that. Leigh Ann Thomas gives perfect-size morsels of goodness for the MOB to digest in an otherwise too-busy-to-eat season of her life. Simply wonderful.

> **~ Eva Marie Everson**
> Author of *Five Brides*
> Tyndale Publishers, 2015

Leigh Ann Thomas has drawn us into her life and the lives of people wanting God to be glorified by the music, Scriptures, words, and worship of a wedding—a living drama telling the story of Christ's return for His Bride.

As Leigh Ann's pastor for almost twenty years, I was always amazed by the way she captured life in a sentence and painted living pictures with her hand movements, with her dramas, and with her true-to-life comedy. *Ribbons, Lace, and Moments of Grace* is a wonderful example of how Leigh Ann can capture a passionate true-to-life story and run your laughter head on into your tears. For twenty years, I enjoyed playing the devil's advocate with this sweet saint of God, not realizing she was taking notes. Indeed, the pen is mightier than the practical joke.

The subtitle of Leigh Ann's book is *Inspiration for the Mother of the Bride*, but this book is for anyone and everyone who loves life and wants to grow closer to God.

~Rev. James Ira Sutton
retired pastor

It's one of those times when you need God's Word the most—your daughter is getting married. Leigh Ann Thomas gives you the Word of God through beautiful and encouraging daily devotions that will walk you through the excitement of picking out the all-important mother-of-the-bride dress to the bittersweet sight of your daughter's empty bedroom. *Ribbons, Lace, and Moments of Grace* helps your relationship with Christ grow through this exciting yet difficult time as you encourage your daughter. You have prayed for this moment your daughter's entire life. Leigh Ann Thomas's work will help you to allow God to use this day to bring glory to Him.

~Rev. Matthew Martin
Pastor of Cool Springs Baptist Church
Sanford, SC

Ribbons, Lace, and Moments of Grace is a reminder to any mother of the bride that in the midst of dress shopping, vendor visits, cake samplings, and the endless list of todos, God is in control and knows a mother's heart. This devotional is a book of great inspiration. Full of wisdom and humor, it can touch and soothe a mother's soul.

~**Mary Lutz**
Certified wedding planner
A Lovely Affair Weddings and Events
alovelyaffairweddings.com

My oldest daughter, Abby, married the love of her life in June 2016. I wish I'd had Leigh Ann's book to guide me through that emotional journey. I read several practical wedding-planning, checklist-type books after Abby and Micah became engaged. I thought I was on top of everything, but nothing truly prepares you for the year leading up to your daughter's wedding—until now.

Leigh Ann's writing is tender and encouraging. She lets you know that you're not going on this journey alone. Her spiritual insights will prove invaluable as you navigate this path. Being the mother of the bride is a privilege; however, it's also one of the most stressful seasons I've ever experienced.

My youngest daughter recently announced her engagement, so I get to be the mother of the bride all over again. Yay! I'm truly grateful that this time around I'll have Leigh Ann's encouraging book in my mother-of-the-bride bag of essentials.

~**Michelle Medlock Adams**
Award-winning writer of over 70 books

In *Ribbons, Lace, and Moments of Grace*, Leigh Ann Thomas captures the tender heart of a mom as she becomes the mother of the bride—the challenges, fears, joys, and soul-aching poignancy. Filled with godly wisdom and heart-tugging stories, it's a beautiful reflection of this special time between a mother and her daughter.

~Michelle Cox
Author of *God Glimpses from the Jewelry Box*
and *Just 18 Summers*

What a moving and inspiring devotional! *Ribbons, Lace, and Moments of Grace* touches a chord with any parent who has experienced the life-altering transition of preparing for a wedding while also preparing to watch their child leave the nest. With both humor and sensitivity, author Leigh Ann Thomas walks mothers through the emotional journey of letting go with grace. I encourage every mother of the bride—and mother of the groom as well—to read this book.

~Elaine Marie Cooper
Author of *Saratoga Letters*

Table of Contents

Acknowledgments

To Hilary Hall—thank you for walking with me through this wonderful, crazy adventure. From idea to completed manuscript, you have encouraged and supported me through every step. Thanks for pushing me to grow and to stretch in my writing. You are an editor extraordinaire and a precious friend. You are loved.

To the incredible women whose stories are in these pages—thank you for showing transparency in how the Lord worked through your mother-of-the-bride journeys. I cherish our one-on-one times as we shared our stories and our hearts. Your prayer support has been my strength and my lifeline. You are treasured friends and beautiful examples of Christ-centered servanthood.

To Denise Loock, Cindy Sproles, and the LPC team—your professionalism and your passion for honoring God with excellence are second to none. Thank you for your vision to reach every person with the life-saving message of Christ. Denise, I am forever thankful for your patience and long-suffering in the editing process. You are amazing.

To my husband and best friend, Roy—thank you for your love, feedback, and support over the last months. Thank you for encouraging me to pursue my writing dreams. You are a man of strength, vision, and godliness. I love you.

To my daughters, Laura, Mary, and Katie—I praise God for the privilege of being your mom. What an adventure to watch you grow and take wing! Thank you for your encouragement and understanding about the times I need to disappear and write. And Laura, thanks for using your gifts of design to help me with my "wedding-ish" one-sheet on this mother-of-the-bride venture.

To my Lord and Savior, Jesus Christ—to You be all glory, honor, and praise. May I never settle for less than Your heart, Your will, and Your purposes. I love You, Jesus.

A Defining Moment

The search had continued for months, and I was struggling. I had to find a dress—The Dress—the perfect mother-of-the-bride garment for the big day. A dress to make me appear a decade younger and at least a few pounds lighter. I exhausted all the major department stores and online outlets and experimented with dozens of styles and colors.

Total tunnel vision: Must. Find. Dress. Now.

The input of friends and family was welcome, but this decision was ultimately mine—one tiny decision in my actual control.

The moment I came face to face with my dream-dress was like a scene from a movie. The store escalator slowly carried me and my hopes upward, depositing me ever so gently in the midst of ladies' formalwear. And there, just steps away, was a headless mannequin adorned in the most gorgeous, shimmery, blue-green garment I had ever seen. It was the only dress I tried on that day because it was The One.

Floating on a cloud of joy, I went home and tucked my newfound treasure into a special corner of the closet, thankful that this particular task could be checked off my list.

Later that week, my mother-in-law found her dress, and she invited me over to share in the excitement. My mother-of-the-bride swagger in place, I walked the short distance to my in-laws' house, stepped inside, and turned to see her wedding day finery.

I'm not sure of the exact series of events, but I have a vague memory of an out-of-body experience. My palms started sweating, and I found it difficult to breathe. I heard voices but not any actual words—only a strange whooshing sound in my ears.

For there, a few steps away, right beside my smiling mother-in-law, was The Dress.

My dress—in all of its blue-green glory.

I sank into a nearby chair while the distant voices asked if I was okay. Murmuring something about having "just jogged over" and being "really out of shape," I made as graceful an exit as possible, every breath an effort on the trek home.

The next week when I recounted the experience to my doctor, he informed me that I had experienced my first panic attack. He smiled and then advised, "Get some rest so you can relax and enjoy the coming family celebration."

Um ... right.

Anyway, my mother-in-law graciously returned her dress and found another she liked even better. For the time being, all was right with the world.

In the ten-month journey of walking with my oldest daughter, Laura, toward her special day, the dress episode was a defining moment for me. I was forced to face many emotions I had set aside in the controlled chaos of wedding planning. Again and again, I went to my heavenly Father and poured out my mother-heart, one full of excitement and joy, fear and anxiety.

One of my babies was getting married, and some things would never ever be the same. My daughter's beautiful middle name, the name I whispered to her at her birth, would slip into obscurity to make way for a new last name.

Our family dynamics would change—from a mom, dad, and three daughters to a family of six, with our first "son." Changes would occur in family vacations, family portraits, and the number of chairs around the dinner table.

Everything in me wanted to yell, "Wait. I'm not ready for this." I wanted to go back in time and whisk my family off to places unknown. I wanted to dig in and keep my little girl my little girl.

Through prayer and daily intake of His Word, the Lord opened my eyes to how I had buried my emotions in a whirlwind of busyness. The life changes on the way were good; they were part of His plans for my daughter's future and for our family. Releasing my worries gave me the freedom and courage to laugh at the mishaps and mayhem that surely lay ahead.

The Lord was growing me. He knew that about a year later, another young man would pull aside my husband, Roy, and me to declare his love for our middle daughter, Mary.

More adjustments and changes.

Through it all, God taught me that this life season was about more than preparing for one special day. This journey was an opportunity to grow in grace and to bring peace and life to my daughters, future sons-in-law, and to others involved in this life-changing event.

My hope is that you and your daughter will delight in each other as you walk the wedding-planning path. As you travel through the pages of *Ribbons, Lace, and Moments of Grace*, my prayer is that God will speak to your heart, providing encouragement, strength, and exceedingly great joy.

Wedding Train of Thought

I can do all this through him who gives me strength.
Philippians 4:13

She's getting married.
Oh my goodness, there's going to be a wedding.
How do I even know where to start?
I'm going to have a son-in-law.
What do I do with a son-in-law?
What will I wear?
I need to lose some weight.
Should I change my hairstyle?
Will I be involved in the planning?
When will we meet his family?

Is my daughter ready to get married?

Have I prepared her for being a wife?

I hope I have time to lose weight.

My baby is getting married.

Lord, help!

The news is official. Face glowing, eyes shining with love, our daughter stands before Roy and me, her hand intertwined with her beloved. As far as the young couple is concerned, no one else exists. Their future is as bright as a Fourth-of-July sky; their dreams have boarded a rocket ship bound for the moon.

The room vibrates with squeals and laughter. Wow, a wedding! This is going to be fun.

Wow. A wedding.

As the sounds of celebration soar around us, a tiny bit of panic seeps in.

Wait. Is this the same little girl who used to burst into the house to share after-school news? The same child who reached for us to bandage a hurting knee or a wounded heart? The same one who promised she would never leave us? That little girl?

We blink. Our daughter stands before us—not the adorable toddler, scrawny preteen, or teenager with braces and bruised knees, but a vibrant, beautiful woman.

Our hearts and our brains struggle to catch up with what has happened in what seems like a matter of moments. Our daughter has grown up and is ready to pledge her life to a man. Joy and expectancy mix with a touch of fear and uncertainty as we work to stay smiling and upbeat.

Can we afford this?

I hope they won't live too far away.

What is Roy thinking right now?

Am I really old enough to be a mother of the bride?

Should we be talking to the preacher and reserving the church?

What in the world do I do now?

And then my gaze touches my daughter's, and she smiles. Her joy floats through the room, wraps around my heart, and gives it a tug. For a moment, the concerns and questions fade, and I'm overwhelmed with the knowledge that God gave Roy and me the honor and privilege of raising this child.

For eighteen plus years, no one has known, loved, or prayed for this person like I have—her mom. I think back to when Roy and I discovered she would become a part of our lives. I never dreamed I could fall in love with someone so quickly.

And just as Mary cradled the baby Jesus in her arms, we pondered and dreamed and envisioned the future with the tiny miracle that God had given us. People watched and smiled and told us that it would "go by so fast."

We didn't believe it for a second. The early days were long, exhausting, and sleep-deprived. It seemed we would be raising children forever. Then it seemed we would be attending recitals, ball games, and youth events forever.

But that whole forever thing was an illusion; now our daughter slips an arm around me and says, "Mom, isn't this awesome? When can we shop for a dress?"

I place my arms around our grown-up bundle-of-joy and hold on tight.

Yes. It is awesome—and exciting and incredible and breathtaking. God has allowed us to be part of yet another milestone in our daughter's life, and with His strength, we'll cherish the journey.

Let the adventure begin.

Father God, only You know the many thoughts fighting for position in my mind. Please give me the strength to begin this life season with calmness and peace. When concerns threaten to engulf me, help me to seek Your wisdom. Thank You, Father, for the privilege of walking with my daughter through this time in her life.

Moment of Grace

Read Psalm 62:2 and reflect on these attributes of God. How does an awareness that God is your rock and your fortress make a difference as you begin the wedding journey with your daughter?

Wait ... What?

Whatever you do, work at it with all your heart, as working
for the Lord, not for human masters.
Colossians 3:23

With one child grown and on her own, one in high school, two more in elementary school, and a full-time position as a fifth-grade teacher, Atha's life was on a super-highway, with few exits leading to those coveted rest areas. Her husband logged a daily two-hour commute, so she bore the weight of the regular household responsibilities.

Then life shifted into overdrive.

One evening in early December, the ring of the telephone echoed through the busy household. Distracted by grading papers and preparations for the next school day, Atha grabbed the phone and said a quick "Hello?"

"Mom, it's me. Guess what? Um, remember Roy? Well, we love each other, and guess what? We're getting married!" (Squeal.)

The stunned mother gripped the phone a bit tighter. *A wedding next summer? How will I get it all together in just over six months?* Then she said, "Wow, that's great, honey. Um, when?"

"Well, I get a few days of leave at Christmas, then I get a few more days between the end of training and when I have to report for duty. So I guess that'll be around the third week in January. We're thinking January 21 would be perfect. Wouldn't a night wedding be so romantic?"

(Insert chirping crickets.)

"Mom? Are you there? We're heading back to the barracks. I have to go. Love you. Can't wait to see you at Christmas!"

Now that I've experienced the wedding process with two of my three daughters, I'm amazed by what this woman, my mom, faced over thirty years ago. But as a flighty, romantic, starry-eyed twenty-one-year-old, I had no clue what I was asking of my bewildered mom.

If I thought it, it must be possible, right?

At that time in my life, anything seemed possible. I'd enlisted in the US Air Force with dreams of traveling the world. But after serving a few weeks, I realized the idea of world travel couldn't compare to the love of the boy back home. Through hundreds of phone calls and handwritten letters, my sweetheart and I decided to tie the knot during the one-week window between the end of my technical training and my report-to-duty date for my first assignment.

I gave my mom one month to pull together the wedding of my dreams. I wanted it all—the flowing dress, my groom in a gray tuxedo, a dozen bridesmaids, an enchanting display of candles and flowers. I wanted an evening of pure magic. "And by the way, Mom, I won't be around to help. I'll fly in three days before the big event. Would you mind pulling it all together?"

In some kind of superwoman effort, my mom accomplished the impossible. With great wisdom, she molded my expectations into something more realistic, but no less beautiful. She planned, schemed, and crafted. She calculated, budgeted, and designed. She gave her oldest, slightly self-absorbed daughter a wedding to remember.

My mom's sacrifices as mother of the bride were a striking reflection of the Savior she continues to serve.

In Ephesians 5:25-27 we read, *Husbands, love your wives, just as Christ loved the church and gave himself up for her to make her holy, cleansing her by the washing with water through the word, and to present her to himself as a radiant church, without stain or wrinkle or any other blemish, but holy and blameless.*

The apostle Paul is writing specifically to husbands, but he's using Christ's love and sacrifice as an example of how to care for a bride. My mom and countless other mothers of the bride have worked and given sacrificially to present their daughters "without stain or wrinkle." Like Christ for His children, mothers pour themselves out in countless ways, reflecting the Savior's love.

My day of magic arrived as I had envisioned—wrapped in flowers, candles, and tiny roses nestled among baby's breath. A dreamy world of pink and gray made possible by an endless storehouse of love.

Selfless mother-love.

From a God-filled heart.

Father, my role in my daughter's wedding seems overwhelming. As we take our first steps toward this special day, help me to remember the loving sacrifices of those who have walked this path before me. May the work of my hands and the attitude of my heart point others to You.

Moment of Grace

Read and meditate on Philippians 2:1-8. How can Christ-centered humility make a difference in your life over the coming months?

But What About...

Do not be anxious about anything, but in every situation,
by prayer and petition, with thanksgiving, present
your requests to God.
Philippians 4:6

he tendency to worry is embedded in a mom's DNA. We look at this child—the one we've reminded to pick up her clothes, to stand straight, and to be on time—and we wonder if we've covered it all.

In the early stages of planning my daughters' weddings, my thoughts often roamed over the previous years of parental instruction. What did I forget to teach?

Have I told her about the joys and responsibilities of being a wife and mother? Is she able to balance a checkbook, stick to a budget, and put together a grocery list? Does she realize how often the bedsheets need changing and the lint trap on the dryer needs cleaning? Will she clean out the back of the refrigerator and mop the floors once in a while? After a few months of wedded bliss, will she wonder why her mom didn't cover all the bases?

What if we're worried about the youth of the happy couple or the completion of their education? From where we stand as parents, we see the wisdom in waiting until after they've graduated from college or nailed down that full-time job. Why not enjoy another birthday or two as a single adult?

And what about this young man grinning his way into the family? How long has he known my daughter? Is he really the one? Will he love, honor, and cherish her forever?

A pastor friend once told me that by the time a couple is sitting in front of him—even if he sees red flags—there's no way to talk them out of their plans. The we-are-so-in-love cloud can overshadow true vision and clear thinking. Rose-colored glasses obscure reality every time.

So if we have genuine concerns, what can we do?

My parents posed the question, "Have you considered getting settled on base for a few months and getting married next summer?"

"No! We want to get married as soon as possible."

My mom and dad never again brought up their concerns. Oh, I'm sure they harbored many fears regarding their oldest daughter. Let's see, she's known him a total of eight months, they dated for less than three of those months, and after the wedding, they'll pull a U-Haul trailer over 2,000 miles from good ole North Carolina to an Air Force base in North Dakota.

North Dakota.

Nope. Nothing to worry about here.

Our first impulse may be to browbeat our children into listening to reason. But I've never heard of a situation where this approach was successful. The finger-in-the-face method can stem the flow of communication with our children.

Most pastors will offer some degree of premarital counseling. If not, a wise parent can offer to seek or to finance sound biblical counsel for the couple. This could be an opportunity to have honest discussions about the future. And what an investment! When our children see that we're voicing concerns from a heart of love and aren't standing in judgment, they'll be more likely to hear us.

Our heavenly Father loves and cares for our children beyond what we could ever imagine. He wants His best for them. When we surrender our anxieties to Him, lay them at His feet, He promises to carry those burdens and to carry us. Our children may choose to take the tougher path. The decision is ultimately theirs. But we can stand close, stand strong, and be consistent as we provide a balance of grace and truth.

The greatest gifts we can give our bright-eyed daughters are fervent prayers, consistent encouragement, and a listening ear. When she knows we are her biggest fan, regardless of her present state of decision-making, she'll trust us when her doubts and questions come.

> *Lord, please help me to think before I speak. Help me to offer expressions of love and encouragement instead of reproach and criticism. And Father, encourage my heart to give You any worries I may have. I love You, Father, and I trust Your heart.*

Moment of Grace

In Revelation 2:1-7, God gives the perfect balance of praise and criticism. Read these verses and reflect on ways to incorporate this same pattern in your role as mother of the bride.

The One

The prayer of a righteous person is powerful and effective.
James 5:16

After raising three girls, having two sons-in-law has been quite the adventure.

My outnumbered husband feels as if he's found life-saving water in an endless desert of estrogen. At last, someone to man-talk while grilling hamburgers and to consult over a car engine or computer hard drive. (I'm not being sexist here. This is the lay-of-the-land in our household.)

It's rather startling to finally meet the men to whom my daughters want to pledge their love, the ones with whom they choose to build a life and raise a family. I watch as my husband sizes each of them up. Are you man enough to love, honor, and cherish my princess? Will you really forsake all others and daily lay down your life for her?

For me, it was more—ah, so it's you. In a between-me-and-God kind of way, it's as if I know them. I've been praying for them for over twenty years. I've prayed that they would be fed and nurtured on the Word of God, that God would keep them safe, and that He'd sanctify each of them for His service. I prayed for depth of character and a desire to seek the will of God. And over the last few years, I've prayed for wisdom to navigate this unique relationship between mother- and son-in-law.

We've all seen the sitcoms depicting the overbearing mother-in-law who thrives on being a thorn in the side of her new son. I didn't want to be that caricature, the butt of society's jokes. The young men my daughters chose already had wonderful moms. Now they were gaining a precious wife. So where did I fit in?

I decided my sons could use another friend and prayer warrior. And what a privilege it is to pray for the spiritual growth and well-being of my daughters' husbands. *And pray in the Spirit on all occasions with all kinds of prayers and requests. With this in mind, be alert and always keep on praying for all the Lord's people* (Ephesians 6:18).

It's a win-win situation.

Taking these men before the Throne of Grace affects their lives, and it reaches my daughters and future grandchildren. Paul wrote, *I urge, then, first of all, that petitions, prayers, intercession and thanksgiving be made for all people* (1 Timothy 2:1). "All people" certainly includes our new sons. God gives the mother of the bride an incredible ministry of intercession—and the joy of touching generations to come.

Sounds like a good fit to me.

Heavenly Father, I come into Your presence to lift up my future son-in-law. I thank You for the joy he has brought to my daughter's life. As they begin their lives together, I pray that he will lead his family in righteousness and that he will seek Your heart in all things. May You guide his heart—shaping, forming, and drawing him into deeper waters with You. I praise You, Father, for Your plans and purposes. In the days to come, enable me to be a source of support and encouragement to this sweet couple. Thank You, Jesus.

Moment of Grace

Read the following verses: Colossians 3:16, Ephesians 4:29, and 1 Peter 4:8-10. Make a list of ways you can be an encouragement for your daughter and future son-in-law.

Dress-Up

I delight greatly in the Lord; my soul rejoices in my God.
For he has clothed me with garments of salvation and
arrayed me in a robe of his righteousness.
Isaiah 61:10

Seeing my daughters Laura and Mary in wedding dresses for the first time was unsettling. In a matter of moments, they transitioned from teens in high-school basketball jerseys to the women before me draped in tulle and beaded lace. The transformation made my head spin.

But after the initial burst of emotion, we settled down and had fun.

Each time one of them emerged from the changing room, she looked like a fairy-tale princess. Once again, I enjoyed seeing my girls play dress-up as they explored the endless glimmering options. They tried on everything, from the ridiculous design to the ridiculous price. Each time they modeled another dress, I paused, waiting to read their expressions. At one point, however, I couldn't help but burst into laughter. Mary appeared wearing a fully hooded, fur-lined cape over her dress. She looked like a female Darth Vader in white.

In the midst of the giggles and playfulness, a touch of oh-my-goodness crept in. So many choices.

A traditional long dress or a tea-length one?

Sheath or mini? (Most definitely not mini.)

Ball gown or A-line?

Trumpet or mermaid?

Sleeves, sleeveless, or strapless?

Veil, hat, or flowers?

Flats or heels?

Hairstyle?

Jewelry?

Getting caught in the tangle of outward adornment can give a mom, or a bride, brain freeze. But I love what God's Word says about it:

Your beauty should not come from outward adornment, such as elaborate hairstyles and the wearing of gold jewelry or fine clothes. Rather, it should be that of your inner self, the unfading beauty of a gentle and quiet spirit, which is of great worth in God's sight. For this is the way the holy women of the past who put their hope in God used to adorn themselves. They submitted themselves to their own husbands, like Sarah, who obeyed Abraham and called him her lord. You are her daughters if you do what is right and do not give way to fear. (1 Peter 3:3-6)

The most beautiful wedding dress in the world won't camouflage inner foulness of spirit. We've invested in our daughter's heart her entire life. Why stop now? Are we praying together through this journey? Are we still encouraging her to nurture the "unfading beauty of a gentle and quiet spirit"? Maybe our daughter hasn't made a decision to live for Christ. Are we even now on our knees before God's Throne of Grace on her behalf?

What an honor to be a mom—to be called to walk alongside our daughters during this special time. But the greatest privilege is the opportunity to lift them up to our heavenly Father and to be a source of encouragement and accountability, guiding them to the beauty that is "of great worth in God's sight."

Father, I treasure the privilege of watching my daughter play dress-up again. Thank You for these moments. Thank You for the gift of this daughter and for the joy she brings to my life. And Father, I pray that she will continue to grow closer to You, that she will seek You in all things. Thank You for Your work in her life. I love You, Jesus.

Moment of Grace

As you meditate on 1 Peter 3:3-6, list specific prayer requests for your daughter. Then add ways you can model the "unfading beauty of a gentle and quiet spirit."

The Perfect Garment

Fine linen, bright and clean, was given her to wear.
Revelation 19:8

On reality television, when brides-to-be say yes to the dress, I sometimes feel sorry for them. They step out on display to friends and family (way too many opinions, if you ask me) and hold their breath, waiting for someone's approval. All too often, a mother, grandmother, or other extended family member clucks her tongue and says no, even when the young woman's heart is already invested. These well-meaning loved ones are turning something sacred into a showcase for their own preferences.

What about us? Are we looking for the dress of our dreams or the one meant for our daughter? Maybe we didn't have a wedding day with all the frills, and we see this wedding as an opportunity for a second chance.

Are we seeking to fulfill our needs at the expense of our daughter's joy? Are we being guided by the weight of regrets? Instead of our daughter's reflection in the dressing-room mirror, are we seeing our own?

Even if the circumstances of our wedding were different from our daughter's and we never had the chance to be adorned in white, the Bible proclaims exciting news: *Let us rejoice and be glad and give him glory! For the wedding of the Lamb has come, and his bride has made herself ready* (Revelation 19:7).

"And his bride has made herself ready." Who is this bride? You and me and all who belong to the Lord Jesus. When Christ comes back for His church, we'll join Him at the wedding supper arrayed in the most exquisite garments ever seen. Pure, fine linen—a material so precious that the gowns in the most upscale bridal boutiques will look like rags.

Our day is coming. But in the meantime, God has an answer for any possible heaviness of heart in this area: He desires *to bestow on them a crown of beauty instead of ashes, the oil of joy instead of mourning and a garment of praise instead of a spirit of despair* (Isaiah 61:3).

When we are tempted to push for our own way, which will lead to a heavy heart, we must put on our own garment, one of God-designed beauty, created especially for us.

A lovely, holy garment of praise.

Lord, thank You for the honor of enjoying this unique journey with my daughter. May our moments together be awash in joy, love, and laughter. And Father, help me to keep my "garment of praise" fresh and wearable so I can be a calm and steady presence over the coming months.

Moment of Grace

After reading Psalm 150, list at least ten personal praises for the blessings your heavenly Father has given you. Rejoice as you reflect on how He continues to work in your life.

Isolation

Cast all your anxiety on him because he cares for you.
1 Peter 5:7

On dress-fitting day, Laura was over-the-top excited. We each drove from several hours away to meet with a seamstress to make sure the wedding dress was perfect. After the fitting, we planned to meet my parents for lunch so Laura and her grandmother could talk about the corsages and boutonnieres.

As I drove to meet my daughter, the sun shone, and a gentle breeze moved the tops of the trees. It was a picture-perfect day. Laura and I were equally excited about the fitting. Likewise, my parents were thrilled to be a part of this special day in the life of their granddaughter. But for some reason, the future mother of the bride couldn't stop crying.

Lord, what's wrong with me? This is exciting. I'm happy, I really am.

I couldn't quite get a handle on the new emotions that resided in my heart. Other moms had walked this wedding path, and they had appeared cool and collected. What was I doing wrong? Why did I feel so sad? I checked my reflection in the rearview mirror. My face was a mess—red and splotchy. Tearstains smudged my makeup. How could I show up looking like this?

Thirty minutes from the meeting point, I pulled into a Dollar General and parked several spaces away from other cars. I leaned back in the seat and released a waterfall of tears. After a while, I pulled on sunglasses and walked into the store searching for new makeup. Fifteen minutes and a new face later, I tugged on a smile and continued my journey. For several months, this became my pattern— cry, cover, continue. I felt overwhelmed and convinced myself that no one else could possibly understand. But I put on a smile and kept moving.

One of Satan's tactics is to convince us that we are alone. If he can push a Christian into isolation, he distances us from one of the greatest resources the Lord has given us—each other.

In my isolation, I attempted to pray and seek God's direction, but I was cutting myself off from His answer.

So many times our Lord works through His people to bring hope and comfort. The apostle Paul encouraged the Galatians to support each other. *Carry each other's burdens, and in this way you will fulfill the law of Christ* (Galatians 6:2). In Psalm 55, David lamented the loss of support and fellowship of a former friend: *with whom I once enjoyed sweet fellowship at the house of God, as we walked about among the worshipers* (v. 14).

By emotionally separating from Christian friends and family, I missed out on the fellowship God designed for me. Maybe other people couldn't understand exactly what I was feeling, but they could reach out with prayers and open arms, arms that represented the loving arms of God.

Father God, help me to remember that if I withhold my heart from Your people, I'll miss so much of Your plan for me. In times of confusion and need, You provide people to encourage, lift up, and support us. Please forgive me for going my own way. When I'm alone and struggling, prompt me to seek wise counsel. I love You, Lord.

Moment of Grace

Write the names of family and friends who could represent the loving arms of God in your life. Pray for the courage to contact them and to ask for guidance and prayer through this unique life season.

Tapping the Money Brakes

Let love and faithfulness never leave you; bind them around
your neck, write them on the tablet of your heart.
Trust in the Lord with all your heart and lean not on
your own understanding.
Proverbs 3:3, 5

According to a popular wedding-planning website, the cost of the average wedding in the good ole USA these days is somewhere north of $30,000. The average in Manhattan swells to over $76,000.[1] Emphasis on the word *average*. When you consider that some couples choose to tie the knot in front of a judge or in a

---

[1] http://money.cnn.com/2015/03/12/pf/planning-for-wedding-costs

family member's living room, expenses on the other end of the money spectrum can easily reach absurdity.

As the bride-to-be flips through her stack of fresh-off-the-press bridal magazines, she can become caught up in the hype. Ads scream out hundreds of must-haves and every-bride-needs-this. The bride finds herself thinking, well, I guess it would be cool to create an outdoor winter wonderland in July—in the South.

You may have seen *Father of the Bride*, a movie that features Steve Martin and Diane Keaton as George and Nina Banks. Their daughter, Annie, gets carried away by her dreams of a spectacular wedding day. Before the financially stunned George can blink, the plans have mushroomed from a small, intimate gathering to an outlandish $250-a-head production. Their family home is remodeled and transformed, tents are set up in the backyard, and swans are rented for the day. And this movie was released in the early 1990s.

No wonder poor George Banks was so stressed. All that hoopla was just for the reception!

The wedding budget is a personal family decision, not a one-size-fits-all. Parents and children need to engage in honest conversation about hopes and expectations. The wedding of her dreams may need to be tempered with a touch of reality. Can you live without swans, doves, and orchids flown in from Hawaii?

Roy and I set a budget and let our daughters live out their dreams within that budget. The decisions were theirs. If they chose to spend extra on flowers and decorations, then another expense category had to be depleted. Our modest budgets were less than a third of the national average, but our girls delighted in evenings of beauty, elegance, and fun. With the help of family and friends, everything came together in celebrations of love and thanksgiving.

As moms, we can help our daughters keep a Christ-centered perspective on their wedding-day expectations. The decisions and preparations leading up to marriage are about so much more than a few hours on a single day. We can encourage our girls to "let love and faithfulness never leave them" and to "trust in the Lord with all their heart."

Without the burdens of overspending and debt, the focus on a daughter's wedding day can center on celebration—God bringing two lives together for the adventure of a lifetime.

Lord, it's so tempting to pour all our resources into preparing for our daughter's big day. I want to give her everything. But Lord, I desire to honor You with our finances. I ask for the courage to draw the line at overspending. Help me to keep Your perspective in all things, and may Your name be glorified.

Moment of Grace
Read Proverbs 3:9 and Luke 14:28-30. Pray and ask God to highlight any areas in the wedding budget that are not honoring to Him.

Waiting in the Wings

Jesus Christ is the same yesterday and today and forever.
Hebrews 13:8

*S*he tried on the peacock-blue dress and "loved it." She modeled the lapis-purple garment, and it was "awesome." She ran errands, set up chairs, and helped to decorate. She used a basketball move and boxed out a dozen other single ladies to claim her oldest sister's bridal bouquet. She smiled for 1,001 pictures and danced until she fell asleep from exhaustion.

With a mix of enthusiasm and quiet contemplation, our youngest daughter, Katie, threw herself into her sisters' big days. My heart squeezed each time she entered the church and walked the aisle ahead of her sister-brides. And when I saw the official wedding pictures from the second big event, I glimpsed things to come. Somewhere between the two weddings, Katie had moved from being Laura and Mary's younger sister, and my baby girl, to a young lady of increasing grace and beauty.

When did this happen? And how was she handling all the changes in our family?

A mother of the bride can easily develop tunnel vision: This is emotional for me; my life is changing; I'm stressed out. But a wedding is a major life transition for the entire family, especially for siblings of the bride.

They watch from the sidelines as their childhood playmates shift their focus from girlhood to adulthood. The big sister they used to hang out with now spends all her time with him—that boy who tags along on family outings and even some vacations. Nothing is the same. All of it can become rather annoying.

"Is he coming with us again?"

The weeks and months invested in planning a wedding can be all-consuming, so staying plugged in to the opinions and feelings of our other children is vital. They long to be involved, but they also want to be reminded of our love and appreciation with hugs, words of encouragement, and scheduled one-on-one time.

Most importantly, we need to remind them of their heavenly Father's unchanging love and faithfulness during the transition. Malachi 3:6 is a powerful truth: *I the Lord do not change.* And Jeremiah 29:11 reminds the siblings of the bride that He has plans and a purpose for them: *"For I know the plans I have for you," declares the Lord, "plans to prosper you and not to harm you, plans to give you hope and a future."*

Our other children may feel that their lives are in a holding pattern while their bridal-sibling experiences real-life adventures. But we can remind them that they are indeed loved, cherished, and valued by the bride, by their family, and by a faithful God.

Father, I thank You and I praise You for each of our children. Over the months of planning, help me to discern when they may need extra time with their mom. Help me to recognize unique opportunities for them to use their gifts and abilities in the planning process. And may I stay sensitive to how each child is adjusting to the changes within our family. Thank You, Jesus, for all the ways You are growing and stretching us in this journey.

Moment of Grace

Praise God for the gifts of your children. Make a list of ways to involve each sibling of the bride in the wedding planning. Then add a few specific ways you can spend one-on-one time with each child during the coming weeks.

The Myth of Smooth Sailing

But the fruit of the Spirit is love, joy, peace, forbearance,
kindness, goodness, faithfulness, gentleness and self-control.
Against such things there is no law.
Galatians 5:22-23

*D*ot gripped the phone in silence. On the other end of the line, someone waited for a response to a question, but the stunned mom didn't quite know how to phrase an answer. She finally managed to stutter, "Um, c-can you repeat that?"

"Yes, of course. My daughter wants to get married on the same day you have the church reserved for your daughter's wedding. Would you mind changing your date or location? My daughter really has her heart set on that church on that day."

Dot blinked. The woman must be kidding. Doesn't she realize my daughter's wedding is only weeks away? Invitations have long been sent, flowers ordered, and myriad schedules changed. The dress is fitted, tuxes rented, and deposits paid for the caterer and photographer. What could this woman be thinking?

My friend Dot said, "No, I'm sorry, but we cannot change our plans."

The caller wasn't happy, but the mother of the bride remained firm. Well, that was strange, she thought. Hopefully, it'll be smooth sailing from here. And for Dot and her family, it was—except for the hailstorm (literally) during the rehearsal dinner that damaged the cars of the wedding party.

Like a hurricane to a long-awaited vacation, a wedding seems to create unique problems and unforeseen circumstances. My daughter Mary's wedding photographer backed out a few weeks before the wedding, and we scrambled to find a replacement. My daughter Laura's caterer was late, and the food wasn't ready when guests arrived.

At my sister Charlene's wedding, my mom and everyone else dealt with a severe ice storm, which caused a power failure that continued from moments before the ceremony through the end of the reception. Another friend arrived on her daughter's big day and discovered the chairs had not been set up at their venue. Dressed in all her mother-of-the-bride glory, she worked to finish the job someone else had neglected, trying not to break into a smelly sweat.

Because we live in an imperfect world, things don't always go as we hope or plan. In fact, we can count on dealing with a few obstacles on our daughter's wedding journey. How do we respond when circumstances change and something doesn't go our way? Do we become tyrants and insist that everyone know how upset we are? Do we risk damaging our Christian witness with our attitude and demeanor?

Wise King Solomon advised, *The end of a matter is better than its beginning, and patience is better than pride. Do not be quickly provoked in your spirit, for anger resides in the lap of fools* (Ecclesiastes 7:8-9). When our plans fail, we may be quickly provoked and say things we'll regret. But others are watching, and not everyone involved in the wedding may be personally acquainted with our Lord and Savior. In fact, their view of Christianity may be influenced by what they see in us.

What an incredible responsibility.

What an amazing privilege.

With the strength and guidance of the Holy Spirit, we can take a step back to think through any situation. We can seek advice and wisdom from trusted friends and family. We can keep a Christ-centered perspective and our sense of humor intact.

Remember Dot's unusual phone call? She received it thirty years ago, but she's still laughing about it and shaking her head in disbelief. During the power outage, my mom scrambled to locate dozens of candles, and my sister had a gorgeous candlelit wedding. Mary's cousin, Grace, stepped up with her camera and took some of our most treasured family photos. Family and friends jumped in during Laura's reception and helped the caterer catch up and complete his obligations. And my friend who set up chairs allowed the Holy Spirit to rule in her heart as she made yet another sacrifice of time and effort for her daughter.

We may not have smooth sailing, but with the fruit of the Spirit, we are guaranteed to have peace in the storm—and a unique story to share.

Wow, Lord, sometimes I wonder what else could possibly go wrong. It seems like our plans continue to get upended and rearranged. When I'm faced with challenging situations, help me to keep my eyes on You. I want my attitudes and actions to reflect Your glory and not my selfishness. Thank You, Lord, for loving me enough to want me to grow and to become more like You. Your patience and loving-kindness astound me. Thank You, Jesus. I love You.

Moment of Grace

Read and meditate on Philippians 4:6-7. What is the best way to guard your heart with the peace of God? List hurdles you've faced on this planning journey. How did you respond? How could you better reflect God's peace and glory the next time an obstacle is placed in your path?

Spanx and the Sausage Keeper

You are altogether beautiful, my darling;
there is no flaw in you.
Song of Songs 4:7

A strange phenomenon happens in the muddled brain of a typical mother of the bride—in this mom's brain, anyway.

I looked in the mirror. Ick. I really am old enough to have a daughter getting married. What can I do to camouflage the signs of the times? Tummy-control undergarments and Oil of Olay are somewhat helpful, but I needed more miracles of modern ingenuity. So I purchased all new makeup (as if that made a difference) and searched for a dress with multiple tiers of fabric to disguise my not-even-close-to-a-twenty-year-old body.

My friend Mary headed straight for the Spanx display at a department store. She found the perfect dress and only needed a touch of smoothing because of the dress's clingy material.

She selected her size, stepped into the dressing room, yanked on the smooth answer-to-her-prayers and got stuck. In the Spanx.

After yanking and tugging for a few minutes, Mary started to sweat, which made the nylon material cling to her skin even more. She squirmed. She wriggled. At some point, her twelve-year-old son asked, "You okay in there?"

On the verge of panic, she thought she might have to wear the undergarment out of the store and hold out the tag for the clerk to scan. Fifteen minutes later, Mary was free and eager to shell out a few bucks for the miracle garment, which she wore on her daughter's big day.

Another friend owned a favorite undergarment that she affectionately called The Sausage Keeper. Knowing it was tucked in the closet when needed, she didn't try it on with her dress until the morning of the wedding.

Big mistake.

The Sausage Keeper was so snug that the back zipper on her dress kept sliding off-center. Each time she gave her dress a yank to straighten it out, it would slide back to the side within minutes. As she stood at the back of the wedding venue, waiting to be escorted in by her future son-in-law, she wasn't praising God for the privilege of walking down the aisle alongside her soon-to-be son. Instead, she was thinking, oh no, my dress is going crooked. Lord, let me make it to my seat!

Even the prophet Samuel got caught up in appearances. The Lord told him to seek out and to anoint the next king of Israel from among the sons of Jesse. Seven of Jesse's sons were impressive—strong, tall, and handsome. Samuel was sure that any one of those who stood before him would be acceptable to the Lord. *But the Lord said to Samuel, "Do not consider his appearance or his height, for I have rejected him. The Lord does not look at the things people look at. People look at the outward appearance, but the Lord looks at the heart"* (1 Samuel 16:7). Instead, the Lord chose Jesse's youngest son, David, to be the future leader of His people. David became a great warrior and a man after God's own heart.

Can we invest in a God-heart and worry less about our appearance? Of course, we want to look our best. Our daughter's wedding is a special day. But it's also the perfect time to let go of every line, crinkle, and bump in our bodies and focus on what God is doing in the lives of His children.

By the time Ms. Spanx, Ms. Sausage Keeper, and I arrived at our respective receptions, all worry had melted away—not just in sweat. We stopped stressing over appearances, pledged to take joy in the moment, and hit the dance floors with abandon. This was a day to celebrate. And besides, our husbands thought we were altogether beautiful.

> *Father, help me to stop worrying so much about my appearance. Give me wisdom to walk through this special time with grace and dignity. And please remind me to invest in what matters—a Christ-centered heart and a life that points to You.*

Moment of Grace

Read Psalm 139 and take note of the ways your Creator treasures you. Commit Psalm 139:14 to memory and lean on this verse when insecurities arise concerning your outward appearance.

There You Go

Love is patient, love is kind. It does not envy, it does not boast, it is not proud.
1 Corinthians 13:4

"How hard can it be? You buy a dress, line up the preacher, and set a date. There you go."

I stood in the church parking lot and stared at my friend as my muddled brain went into overdrive. There you go? Are you kidding me? Do you have anyone to invite? Do you plan on feeding them? Wouldn't it be nice to have a few pictures of the event? Do you want flowers? What kind? How about candles or music? Do you plan on grabbing a guitar and heading to the backyard? Which is fine, but …

My thoughts were on a rampage, but I just smiled. My dear never-been-a-mother-of-the-bride friend didn't mean any harm. In fact, I found myself wondering, how hard can it be? Another day found me sitting in my car crying into my cell phone. And another friend said, "My goodness, what's wrong? Did they call off the wedding?"

In between sobs, I managed to stutter, "N-no. It's just that she's getting m-married."

The silence on the phone went on so long that I checked to see if my friend was still there. She finally said, "Um, I'm sure it'll be all right. Talk to you later?"

After several situations where I felt like a loon around certain people, it hit me. If you haven't personally experienced being a mother of the bride, it's impossible to fully grasp its emotional magnitude.

Friends try to understand. They can sympathize, but they can't identify.

That's the way it is in our spiritual life too. The things of Christ are spiritually discerned. We can talk about our Christ-life to our unsaved friends ad nauseam. But unless they respond to the work of the Holy Spirit and experience a relationship personally, they'll never grasp the depth of Christ's love and sacrifice. Why? *The person without the Spirit does not accept the things that come from the Spirit of God but considers them foolishness, and cannot understand them because they are discerned only through the Spirit* (1 Corinthians 2:14).

They don't have the precious deposit of the Holy Spirit to give them understanding. *Because you are his sons, God sent the Spirit of his Son into our hearts, the Spirit who calls out, "Abba, Father"* (Galatians 4:6).

My experiences with these other moms were God's gentle reminder to show calmness and compassion with those who can't understand the ways of God because they lack spiritual discernment. There's no room for frustration when I perceive in others a lack of interest or understanding in the message of the cross. The Holy Spirit does the work of wooing and redeeming the hearts of His people.

How beautiful and freeing!

Now, there you go.

Father, help me to see that even though others can't fully understand this journey, they can still be a source of comfort and encouragement. Help me to be patient and kind. And Father, for those who don't know You, I pray for the work of Your Spirit in their lives. May I never be a hindrance to Your work and power. Help me to always direct the glory to You.

Moment of Grace

Reflect on the fruit of the Spirit mentioned in Galatians 5:22-23. How can a close walk with the Lord make a difference when you interact with those who don't understand your wedding journey?

I've Got the Joy

*You make known to me the path of life; you will fill me with
joy in your presence, with eternal pleasures at your right hand.*
Psalm 16:11

Carly sat across from her daughter and future
son-in-law and waited for a response. Her two previous
questions had faded away unnoticed, and it seemed that
her latest query was doomed to the same fate. Gazes
locked, the giddy twosome whispered and giggled,
oblivious to anyone else in the restaurant, including the
loved ones sitting at their table.

Carly sighed. She did a lot of that these days. And in
that sigh swirled conflicting emotions. She was excited

about her daughter's upcoming nuptials. She already loved her son-to-be. And most of the time, she enjoyed watching their adoration for each other.

But today, seeing their loving looks and intertwined fingers filled Carly's heart with an odd ache. Something about their joy, expressed in giggles and loving glances, made her feel old. Dry. Used up. Her heart squeezed as the realization washed over her: I'm jealous of their joy.

Oh, she was thankful for her marriage of 30 years and counting, but at the moment, it looked quite different from the glow of the starry-eyed couple across from her. Carly found herself praying, "Lord, why can't I be a part of this? Why can't I experience this joy?"

She then heard a still small voice within her spirit. "Child, where is your joy in Me?"

Her heart tightened again, but this time with conviction. In the days and weeks of wedding busyness, her most vital relationship had slipped out of first place. For the first time in a long time, Carly felt the stirrings of hope. Oh Father, she thought, I need to rejoice in You. Then I can really be a part of my daughter's joy.

Our Lord was teaching this mother of the bride to find her fulfillment in Him alone. As she allowed Christ to reach in and restore the neglected recesses of her heart, His Living Water seeped into all the dry, cracked places. *For you make me glad by your deeds, Lord; I sing for joy at what your hands have done. How great are your works, Lord, how profound your thoughts!* (Psalm 92:4-5).

When we lock our gaze with that of the King of Kings and remember our First Love, the Lord of Lords, we are free to participate in the wedding bliss around us. We are able to truly say, "I sing for joy at what Your hands have done."

Oh Father, how amazing You are. How beautiful and faithful! Thank You for restoring in me the joy of my salvation. You are my hope and my righteousness, and my fulfillment is found in You alone. I will praise You in song and dance. I will praise You with my life.

Moment of Grace

Immerse yourself in the joyful words of Psalm 47:1-3 and Psalm 71:23. Take time each day to praise God for the joy of your salvation.

Trust and Verify

If we are faithless, he remains faithful,
for he cannot disown himself.
2 Timothy 2:13

*L*ynn glanced at her watch as she drove through the entrance of the luxury complex. Bridal portrait day had finally arrived. The photographer had made the arrangements and provided her and her daughter with the location and meeting time. She felt a rush of excitement as she smiled at the bride-to-be in the passenger seat. Mother and daughter had spent hours in preparation for this appointment.

Even off-season, the venue was beautiful. A historic white-columned inn stood tall and stately in a pastoral setting of rolling hills. Brick pathways meandered past towering oaks and foliage-trimmed fountains. The setting exuded Southern charm and elegance. Lynn was thrilled that her daughter's pictures would be taken in such beauty.

They found a parking spot near the massive inn and made their way inside where the grandeur continued. Crystal pitchers and glassware adorned tables in a room anchored with an immense fireplace from another era. Lynn felt a bit out of her element, but she was eager to begin the portrait session. Not seeing anyone to check them in, and still waiting for the photographer, mother and daughter located a groundskeeper who provided access to a room for the bride to change into her dress.

Some time later, the photographer arrived, and for the next few minutes, Lynn and her daughter enjoyed both the moment and their lovely surroundings. As they walked through the well-kept grounds, the photographer took pictures; each one captured another special moment.

Then they heard an unfamiliar voice: "Excuse me, but may I ask what you're doing? Do you have an appointment?"

Lynn smiled and nodded toward her daughter and the photographer. "We're taking my daughter's bridal portrait."

The professionally dressed woman was undeterred. "But do you have an appointment?"

Stunned, Lynn glanced at the photographer, waiting for her to affirm the appointment. But she remained silent.

After a few moments, Lynn stammered, "Um, I thought, I mean, I didn't realize—"

"People pay a lot of money to have pictures taken here," the other woman said. "If you don't have an appointment, then you're trespassing. You'll have to leave."

The still-silent photographer gave a shrug and began to gather her equipment.

Lynn was mortified. "I'm so sorry. We'll leave right away."

The surrounding beauty faded as mother and daughter scrambled to collect their belongings and leave before they encountered any more trouble.

Lynn learned a vital wedding and planning lesson: double- and triple-check the reputation and experience of your wedding vendors. A creative, sparkling website does not a professional make. This vendor made promises she couldn't uphold, and her excuses were unacceptable.

Thankfully, this mother of the bride didn't place her wedding hopes and expectations on the reliability of her vendors. Lynn's feet were firmly planted in the Word of God. His promises were nestled in her heart and mind: *Know therefore that the Lord your God is God; he is the faithful God, keeping his covenant of love to a thousand generations of those who love him and keep his commandments* (Deuteronomy 7:9). *For the word of the Lord is right and true; he is faithful in all he does* (Psalm 33:4).

Lynn was aggravated and annoyed with the stressful events but not swept away.

Sometimes we may wonder if we can depend on anyone, if being faithful and true is a virtue of the past. Praise God, we can lean with confidence on His Word and His promises because, on the cross, Christ proved the extent of His love and faithfulness.

No further verification needed.

Father, I praise You for Your faithfulness. When the world is a cloud of chaos around me, You are my rock and my refuge. Thank You for keeping Your promises and for being my sure foundation.

Moment of Grace

Meditate on the following verses: Hebrews 13:8, Malachi 3:6, Isaiah 40:28-31, and 2 Timothy 2:13. When others let us down, how can these verses remind us of the stability we have in Christ?

Attitude of Gratitude

*Give thanks in all circumstances; for this is God's
will for you in Christ Jesus.*
1 Thessalonians 5:18

*S*arah and I relaxed as we sat in a local sandwich shop, entertaining each other with our mother-of-the-bride escapades. After a good hour of laughter and jokes over shared memories, my friend grew quiet.

"You know, Leigh Ann, so many things in my daughter's wedding journey mirrored my walk with Christ."

I nodded in agreement. God had also worked in my life in unique ways throughout my daughters' wedding journeys. But because we serve a creative, personal God, I was eager to hear Sarah's unique story and to glean encouragement from her experiences.

Sarah explained how she had certain expectations as she planned a special trip for the bride and her bridesmaids. On day two of the weekend getaway, Sarah realized she was being excluded from most activities and conversations. She felt more like a chauffeur and event planner than a cherished mother of the bride.

"There I was, watching them chatter away, oblivious to my irritation. I was thinking, I paid for lunch, I drove the car, and I made all the arrangements. Don't these girls realize the sacrifices I've made? How can they exclude me? Then regret poured through me. In an instant, I was reminded of my Lord's sacrifices for me and how I'm so guilty of taking His love for granted.

"These young women were vaguely aware of how I made the weekend possible, but they had no clue about the details. In contrast, I am personally acquainted with Someone who gave His life for me. I'm fully aware of His sacrifice and yet"—Sarah's eyes filled with tears—"Jesus endured shame and punishment for me, but sometimes I go days without saying, 'Thank You.' I exclude Him from life decisions. I take Him for granted."

God worked in Sarah's life to draw her closer to Himself and to reflect the glory of His Son. In turn, her shared experience was a reminder for me and for future mothers of the bride.

In his letter to the Colossian church, Paul writes, *And whatever you do, whether in word or deed, do it all in the name of the Lord Jesus, giving thanks to God the Father through him* (Colossians 3:17). In previous verses, Paul teaches about the peace of Christ and the exercise of thankfulness. Then he wraps a huge bow around those teachings by exhorting us to give our all in whatever we do—completely, wholeheartedly, and joyfully.

Sacrifice is part of the journey.

Our daughters may not always show their gratitude. But with God's strength and wisdom, we can show the forgiveness and patience that our Lord extends to us.

Abba, Father, thank You for Your never-ending forbearance and forgiveness. I'm so ashamed of how I've been wrapped up in my own thoughts and self-interest. When irritations crowd in and try to rob me of peace, help me to remember Your great love and sacrifice. Help me to keep a Christ-centered heart in all things. Thank You, Jesus.

Moment of Grace

Read Psalm 100 and reflect on ways to praise God in spite of circumstances. When you feel unappreciated, how can a thankful heart give you a Christ-centered perspective?

Too Much of a Good Thing?

A gentle answer turns away wrath, but a harsh word stirs up anger.
Proverbs 15:1

A wedding brings families and friends together.

For extended periods of time.

In small spaces.

The night before the wedding ceremony, one friend housed not only her immediate family but also all the groom's attendants. She played hostess until the early hours of the wedding-day morning, then got up early to provide breakfast for everyone before she rushed to the wedding venue to check on table arrangements.

Another friend was shadowed for days by someone's Aunt So-and-so. No one seemed to remember how she was related to the family. This pint-sized woman, with long, white hair, simply stood and stared at the festivities, never saying a word. A couple of days after the wedding, she vanished. My friend gets a case of the "creepies" just thinking about it.

One bewildered mother of the bride struggled to hold herself together when an extended family member cried because she didn't have a corsage to wear during the ceremony. The explanation of "just the moms and the wedding party have special flowers" didn't matter. Eventually, someone gave up her own flowers to appease the demanding woman.

A wedding tends to bring out the best—and the worst—in people.

Think about it. Two families, who may or may not know each other, will be forever joined by the pledge of love between one man and one woman. Over the following years, they will likely share get-togethers and grandchildren. Everyone involved wades through these uncharted waters, and the resulting tensions surface in various ways.

Aunt Edna wants a designated seat at the ceremony.

Cousin Bertie is still sulking because she's not a bridesmaid.

The adorable twin flower girls have never had a moment's discipline in their lives. You fantasize about throwing them out a window.

Whatever the challenges, God's Word offers wisdom for these wedding irritations.

In the first chapter of Colossians, Paul encourages the believers to honor the Lord in their lives and to please Him by bearing good fruit:

> *We continually ask God to fill you with the knowledge of his will through all the wisdom and understanding that the Spirit gives, so that you may live a life worthy of the Lord and please him in every way: bearing fruit in every good work, growing in the knowledge of God, being strengthened with all power according to his glorious might so that you may have great endurance and patience, and giving joyful thanks to the Father* (Colossians 1:9-12).

Praise God that His Spirit gives wisdom and understanding. At times, a mother of the bride needs "great endurance and patience" so she can bear good fruit and not launch an apple or two at Cousin Bertie and Aunt So-and-so.

> *Lord, when I'm tempted to be unkind because of the perceived slights of others, help me to remember Your limitless love and restraint. Don't let my witness become*

watered down by my responses to petty irritations. Thank You, Father, for Your forgiveness. Help me to keep my eyes on You.

Moment of Grace

In Ephesians 4:31-32, God commands us to "get rid of all bitterness, rage, and anger." How do the closing words in verse 32 make this possible?

Sync Up, Suit Up!

Finally, be strong in the Lord and in his mighty power.
Put on the full armor of God.
Ephesians 6:10-11

We were a few days out from the big day, and this mom was on fire.

Working from a to-do list that resembled a small book, I tackled each item in record time. I worked the phone like a pro. I double-checked tables and seating areas at the reception site. I confirmed linen rentals. My Camry and I zipped through a dozen errands, stopping only to refuel when the needles on our gas gauges hovered over the neon E.

I was organized. I was purpose driven. I was steeped in an I've-got-this mentality that bordered on cockiness. See the foreshadowing of a meltdown?

But in spite of my abundant energy and pure intentions, by mid-afternoon I was running on emotional fumes, close to tears. Frustrated, I whined, "Lord, I don't understand. What's wrong with me? I'm working hard and accomplishing so much. Why do I want to cry and hit something?"

I groaned as I realized my mistake—a misstep I've made too many times to count.

I had left my suit of armor at home, sitting by the back door.

Paul writes in Ephesians 6:14-17: *Stand firm then, with the belt of truth buckled around your waist, with the breastplate of righteousness in place, and with your feet fitted with the readiness that comes from the gospel of peace. In addition to all this, take up the shield of faith, with which you can extinguish all the flaming arrows of the evil one. Take the helmet of salvation which is the word of God.*

On this supercharged day, I short-cut my time with the Lord. I had things to do, mountains of tasks to accomplish. Surely it would be okay to skip time in the Word on this one day. Time was a-wastin'!

In my zeal, I neglected to sync up with my source of strength and power. I know my smartphone and other gadgets won't make it more than a day with one charge. Why do I expect my heart and mind to skip a day? I assumed that yesterday's power would push me through today's challenges. Instead, I ended up anxious and frustrated. Any ordinary day can usher in myriad hiccups and hurdles. Add some mother-of-the-bride tension, and the potential for detonation veers toward high alert.

God's Word has much to say about syncing up with our Lord. *Look to the Lord and his strength; seek his face always* (1 Chronicles 16:11). *Ask and it will be given to you; seek and you will find; knock and the door will be opened to you. For everyone who asks receives; the one who seeks finds; and to the one who knocks, the door will be opened* (Matthew 7:7-8).

Do you need strength? Ask.

Do you need wisdom and discernment? Seek.

Do you long to know and follow the heart of God? Knock.

So let's sync up, suit up, and lift up praise to God for His never-ending power.

Lord, I confess my neglect of Your Word. I have tried to live in my feeble strength and power instead of depending on You. Thank You for extending forgiveness, grace, and compassion to this deeply flawed woman. And thank You for loving me enough to draw me back to You.

Moment of Grace

Review the last few days of wedding planning. Are you setting aside time to sync up and recharge in God's Word? What adjustments do you need to make so time with the Lord becomes a priority?

Silver and Gold

A cord of three strands is not quickly broken.
Ecclesiastes 4:12

*W*hen my daughters were young, I became used to hearing the words, "Mommy, I can do it by myself." My independent cherubs preferred to tackle certain tasks without me, such as preparing their lunches or deciding what to wear for the day.

I did my best to step back and wait until I was needed. While I waited, I noticed that my preschoolers struggled to ask for help. In their naïve minds, they didn't need me—until frustration set in when they felt overwhelmed.

Their attitude mirrors that of a typical mother of the bride. We can do this. We're intelligent women who've given birth and raised a family. We've conquered potty training, puberty, and teenage angst. We've managed a household for years. We're the ultimate multitaskers. This wedding thing is one event. Why would we need help?

Solomon, the wisest man who ever lived, gives this advice: *Two are better than one, because they have a good return for their labor: If either of them falls down, one can help the other up. But pity anyone who falls and has no one to help them up* (Ecclesiastes 4:9-10).

Dottie recalls the days leading up to her daughter's wedding: "Thinking about the reception was stressful. Would there be enough food? Did we remember everything? I can't imagine those days without the friends who stepped in to help with the details. They took away a lot of the stress."

Kay is grateful for the Lord's work in her life. He convicted her heart and gave her the strength to become more transparent. Initially, it was hard to let others help, but the physical assistance and the emotional support were priceless. By accepting support, Dottie and Kay experienced a "good return for their labor." Loving hands helped to carry their burdens and to uplift their spirits.

A Google search on "mother of the bride" yields an endless list of advice, mostly about what to wear and a recommended checklist of things to accomplish. But don't overlook one of the most vital resources—friends.

If we'll pause and look around, we'll discover that God's provision is amazing.

Don't know how to arrange a coffee bar for the reception?

Unsure of where to start shopping for wedding essentials?

Feeling a bit weighed down with details?

God calls us to seek wise counsel and godly friendships. In fact, assembling a team of prayer warriors is the smartest thing a mother of the bride can do. Knowing that someone is taking us before the Throne of Grace can make all the difference. *Therefore encourage one another and build each other up, just as in fact you are doing* (1 Thessalonians 5:11). *Perfume and incense bring joy to the heart, and the pleasantness of a friend springs from their heartfelt advice* (Proverbs 27:9).

Can this wedding journey seem all-consuming? Depending on the day or moment—yes. But God provides through His Word, His Holy Spirit, and through the "pleasantness of a friend."

Oh Father, thank You for the gifts of friendship that You have given me. I'm overcome with gratitude for their support, wisdom, and guidance. Thank You for using them to corral my scattered thoughts and to provide much-needed stability. I ask for Your blessings on their lives.

Moment of Grace

Write the names of the friends God has given you and the specific ways they help you. Thank Him for their influence and support during this time in your life.

The Anchor Holds

We have this hope as an anchor for the soul.
Hebrews 6:19

I leaned against the wall of the women's room and tried to slow my breathing. Mary, her fiancé, and I had sampled food for her reception, and I was having an allergic reaction to something I had eaten. Light-headed and sweaty, I prayed with urgency: "Lord, oh please don't let me pass out in a public restroom."

Kay inhaled a breath of below-freezing January air, stepped over a cow patty, and tried to calm herself. As her daughter's wedding gown dragged through the cow pasture, she couldn't help but moan. Thoughts stampeded through her mind: Her dress is going to be ruined. Are we out of our minds? A bridal portrait session in a field? It's so cold her lips are turning blue.

From her official seat in the church sanctuary, Mary Lynn's eyes widened in alarm as the flower girl in her daughter's wedding gagged into her flower basket. As the wedding party bowed for prayer, she whisked the child offstage and handed her to another relative. Sick from nerves, the tiny attendant missed the entire ceremony.

Sylvia watched in shock as her daughter passed out cold during her portrait session. Rushing to her daughter's side, she yelled for the photographer to do something. The seasoned wedding photographer just shook his head. He had seen it many times before.

On this mother-of-the-bride journey, we encounter unusual situations and become entangled in circumstances we never imagined. As we work to prepare a day of magic for our daughters, possibilities such as cow patties, nauseated flower girls, and bridal fainting spells never enter our minds.

Even when we're not involved in a wedding, we face a minefield of hazards—job loss and relocation, loss of loved ones, financial stress, and sickness. Sometimes it feels as if the ground has shifted beneath our feet. As we struggle to maintain our balance, we look for something or someone to grasp.

And that's when we reach for the Anchor.

The writer of Hebrews encouraged the Christians in Palestine to "take hold of the hope" set before them. The Christian walk was difficult, so he reminded the early Christ-followers of how to be steadfast. *God did this so that, by two unchangeable things in which it is impossible for God to lie, we who have fled to take hold of the hope set before us may be greatly encouraged. We have this hope as an anchor for the soul, firm and secure* (Hebrews 6:18-19).

As mothers of the bride, we can be a steady presence in the lives of our daughters and others involved in the wedding. We all have an anchor, either our own strength or the strength of the Living God. Unusual circumstances in our daughter's wedding journey may be inconsequential compared to other, sometimes severe life events. But even those times that we later recall with laughter and a shake of the head can seem overwhelming when we first encounter them.

Our Lord is always present in the lives of His people. And when we find ourselves upside down in unexpected situations, He beckons us to reach for Him, the Anchor firm and secure.

Precious Father, when I'm tempted to become engulfed by circumstances, convict my heart, so I'm compelled to reach for You. Help me to remember that You are my anchor and my sure foundation. You alone provide me with peace and strength. Thank You, Father, for Your steady presence in my life.

Moment of Grace

In Luke 6:47-49, Jesus explains the consequences of a weak foundation. What steps can you take today to strengthen your foundation in Christ? How can you encourage the engaged couple to begin their marriage on solid ground?

Breaking Bad

*May these words of my mouth and this meditation of my
heart be pleasing in your sight, Lord,
my Rock and my Redeemer.*
Psalm 19:14

I stood near our church office and stared at my pastor. Teasing me about being a stressed-out mom, he had said something like this: "Weddings would go a lot smoother if mothers would stay out of it and just show up on the wedding day."

Any other time, I would have laughed and shrugged off his comments. The two of us had a history of good-natured joking, and I knew he didn't mean what he said.

But this wasn't any other time. Laura's wedding was only weeks away, and I felt the mounting pressure of being ready. I glared at him, raised my voice a few decibels, and spit out, "Well, I'd like to know how things would get done without the mom."

Amused, he sparred back, unaware of my fragile state of mind.

I don't remember my exact response, but it was harsh. I turned and headed for the exit because I didn't want him to witness my torrent of tears. Aghast at my tone, and fighting back the rising flood, I realized what I had done. I had snapped at my pastor.

Snapped.

At my pastor.

Surely I had broken the eleventh commandment: Thou shalt not, under any circumstances, be rude to your minister, for in the day that you do, you shalt surely die.

I wish I could say the episode was an isolated event, but I'd be breaking another commandment if I did. No, I don't remember insulting our minister again, but there were other times when I couldn't believe the words that fell from my lips.

No good tree bears bad fruit, nor does a bad tree bear good fruit. Each tree is recognized by its own fruit. People do not pick figs from thornbushes, or grapes from briers. A good man brings good things out of the good stored up in his heart, and an evil man brings evil things out of the evil stored up in his heart. For the mouth speaks what the heart is full of (Luke 6:43-45).

"For the mouth speaks what the heart is full of."

My heart was crammed with tension, worries, and stress. There was no room for the perfect peace of my heavenly Father. The encounter with my pastor revealed a deeper problem. My words spilled out of a heart overflowing with frustration, fatigue, and self. When the stress began to build, I should have breathed the prayer of the psalmist in Psalm 141:3—*Set a guard over my mouth, Lord; keep watch over the door of my lips.*

I love this verse because I visualize a tiny guard standing watch beside my mouth, sword in hand, ready to attack any unseemly words that try to slip out. When I neglect time in prayer and in God's Word, however, my guard becomes lethargic and abandons his post.

Never a good thing.

As mothers of the bride, may we maintain an attitude of prayer and lean with confidence on the power of the Holy Spirit. Our pastors and everyone else involved in this life event will appreciate it.

Lord, at times I'm ashamed of my attitudes and actions. When I'm stubborn and wrapped up in myself, I am humbled by Your endurance and longsuffering. Thank You for Your forgiveness and restoration. Father, I long to be led by Your Spirit. Please make me more like You.

Moment of Grace

Read James 1:26, then review your words and actions over the last days and weeks. Ask God to show you areas where forgiveness and restoration are needed. Praise Him for His mercy and grace.

Heart of a Servant

[Abigail] bowed down with her face to the ground and said,
"I am your servant and am ready to serve you and wash the
feet of my lord's servants."
1 Samuel 25:41

Family and close friends, both men and women, gathered in a circle to honor the engaged couple with a shower of love, encouragement, and gifts. Joy and laughter floated through the room as they offered inspiration and prayers for the couple's future.

After a few minutes, the circle of loved ones stopped their chatter and paused in quiet anticipation. The bride's parents felt God leading them to give their daughter and future son-in-law a visual reminder of the foundation of a Christ-centered marriage.

With a heart full of love, Mary Lynn, the bride's mother, began reading aloud from the gospel of John:

Jesus knew that the Father had put all things under his power, and that he had come from God and was returning to God; so he got up from the meal, took off his outer clothing, and wrapped a towel around his waist. After that, he poured water into a basin and began to wash his disciples' feet, drying them with the towel that was wrapped around him. He came to Simon Peter, who said to him, "Lord, are you going to wash my feet?" Jesus replied, "You do not realize now what I am doing, but later you will understand." "No," said Peter, "you shall never wash my feet." Jesus answered, "Unless I wash you, you have no part with me." (John 13:3-8)

A holy stillness filled the room during the Scripture reading as Mary Lynn's pastor-husband kneeled at her feet with a pitcher and basin. She felt the warm water and the warmth of her husband's hands; with gentleness and reverence, this godly man served his wife by washing her feet.

Overcome with emotion, Mary Lynn marveled at God's presence in the moment. She thought, I can't believe he's washing my feet. Oh Lord, thank You for what You are doing.

Her husband then took a cloth and dried his wife's feet. They were precious feet that had walked beside him through a lifetime of ministry, feet that had walked a sacrificial path for him and their children, but mostly for their Lord. Always for their Lord.

Still kneeling, he read words penned from their parent-hearts: "We believe sacrificial servanthood that issues forth from Christ-like humility is the key to a godly marriage. Jesus spoke of His love for His disciples and all people often. He always lived out that love in sacrificial giving. The ultimate act of His servanthood was His obedient death on the cross for our sins. A few hours before He died on the cross, the God of the universe washed the feet of His disciples. Jesus knew that we humbly serve those whom we truly love. Fill your days with acts of humble service to each other and to a world that needs to see Christ's love lived out in you."

This mother and father engraved a sacred image on the hearts of a couple beginning their walk of love and sacrifice. With a simple act, they modeled their Lord's desire for His people to love with extravagance and selflessness.

What a beautiful reminder for us to love sacrificially, not only our families but also the world around us. We easily become swept away by our all-about-me culture. But God calls us to deeper, authentic living—a life that embraces His heart and shares it with those He places along our path.

Praise God that He doesn't leave us wallowing in self; instead, He offers us the gifts of abundance and deeper joy.

Father God, once again I stand amazed by Your call to love and serve You with all that I am. Give me strength to love my family and others sacrificially. May I seek to model Your examples of loving and giving with genuine humility. And may my feeble efforts bring glory and honor to Your Name.

Moment of Grace

Reflect on the story in John 13 of Jesus washing the feet of His disciples. Imagine sitting there as your Lord kneels before you as if He were a servant. How does that image alter your perspective on this wedding journey?

A Striking Resemblance

The Son is the radiance of God's glory and the exact repre-
sentation of his being, sustaining all things by his powerful
word. After he had provided purification for sins, he sat
down at the right hand of the Majesty in heaven.
Hebrews 1:3

Mary and I met for a day of pre-wedding shopping, and we meandered through the mall near her college campus. We had plenty to talk about. Many details were covered, but just as many were yet to be tackled. Our church was being renovated, so the wedding would be held at the groom's church, a couple of hours from our home. Extra travel, long-distance coordination, hotel arrangements for the wedding party and assisting with out-of-town guests were all part of her wedding equation.

The big day was still a few months away, so we felt no sense of urgency. We relished the opportunity to spend time together as mother and daughter. I enjoyed walking beside the girl who had grown into a beautiful grown-up girl, ready to pledge her love to her sweetheart.

Then the day became even better.

We looked for an available register to make our purchases. As we approached the salesclerk, a smile spread across the woman's face. I almost looked over my shoulder to see if she was looking at someone else. As we neared her, she grinned even bigger and said, "Wow! You two have to be mother and daughter."

This mom will never forget that moment. A stranger thought that my daughter and I favored each other. So much so, that the salesclerk's face glowed with excitement when she spoke of it.

I glanced at Mary to see her response to the woman's enthusiasm and was pleased to see my daughter smiling. For my part, I was thrilled. Are you kidding me? This salesclerk sees a resemblance between me and my fit and trim twenty-two-year-old daughter? Lady, are you working on commission? Because if you are, I'll buy anything you place in front of me right now.

The experience made me think of someone else I'm supposed to favor—my heavenly Father. As I reflected on that treasured moment with my middle daughter, I wondered if others see a reflection of my Lord when they look at me. Am I a mirror image of His glory or a tarnished version clouded with self-glory?

If the salesclerk had seen Mary and me on separate occasions, she wouldn't have noticed that we looked alike. She saw a resemblance between us because we were walking side by side. *Follow God's example, therefore, as dearly loved children and walk in the way of love, just as Christ loved us and gave himself up for us as a fragrant offering and sacrifice to God* (Ephesians 5:1-2). *Whoever claims to live in him must live as Jesus did* (1 John 2:6).

"Walk in the way of love."

"Live as Jesus did."

If we're not walking with Christ, if we've veered off on our own path, others won't see His reflection in us.

And what joy we miss.

How thrilling it would be to hear someone say, "You two have to be Father and daughter. You look just like Him."

Wow, Lord. Thank You for this special day and for reminding me to walk beside You. May my greatest joy come from reflecting You in the way I live. Thank You, Father, for the privilege of placing my hand in Yours. I love You, Jesus.

Moment of Grace

Meditate on Ephesians 5:1-2 and 1 John 2:6. How are your actions and attitudes a reflection of the Savior you serve?

Really, Lord?

But in your hearts revere Christ as Lord. Always be
prepared to give an answer to everyone who asks you to
give the reason for the hope that you have.
But do this with gentleness and respect.
1 Peter 3:15

The last few days had been exasperating. One of
our wedding vendors was being … difficult.

I had trouble pinpointing when the trouble began.
Initial phone contacts were fine. But our first face-to-face
meeting was awkward, the conversation stilted. I thought
she might have had a tough day. Her work samples
were beautiful and professional, so with my daughter's

blessing, I signed on the dotted line and handed over the required deposit.

The deposit is an anchor to the good, but it becomes a ball and chain to the not-so-good. Over time, we discovered we were locked into a business relationship with someone who took no pleasure in her work or relationship to her clients. Her words were cutting and rude. We joked that she must be anti-marriage (unusual for someone who earned their living in the wedding industry).

My instinct was to confront. We were paying good money for her talents, and we didn't deserve the rude treatment. But as the days passed, my morning Scripture readings kept replaying in my heart and mind. *Be prepared to give an answer*, Peter advised. *Make the most of every opportunity*, Paul instructed (Colossians 4:5).

"But Lord," I countered. "She's not very nice."

Show her Me.

The Holy Spirit's directive was clear. This vendor was not behaving in a professional manner, but my call to action was not contingent on her behavior. Who knew what battles this woman was fighting?

No, I didn't need added stress during my daughter's wedding journey. But God had allowed these circumstances, so there had to be a way to glorify Him in them. Remember that annoying verse in Romans? You know the one: *And we know that in all things God works for the good of those who love him, who have been called according to his purpose* (Romans 8:28).

All things. For the good.

Did God bring this woman to us so she could witness the true love and joy of a Christian wedding? Was God using her presence and involvement to refine me into a more loving, compassionate person?

Perhaps yes—to both questions.

A few minutes before the ceremony began, the vendor snapped at both my daughter and me. I opened my mouth to return her rudeness, but I caught the eye of my daughter-bride. She smiled and said, "Mom, it's okay."

And in that moment, in the midst of my daughter's joy, it was okay. God was present in the day and in the joining of two people in the covenant of a lifetime. By responding with gentleness and respect, our witness remained intact, and our Lord was glorified.

Lord, when other people are rude, help me to pause and to think before I respond. Give me the wisdom to see others through Your eyes, not through a veil of irritation. I pray for strength to show compassion in this journey. And Father, may my actions and speech reflect Your heart, not mine.

Moment of Grace

How can the wisdom found in 2 Timothy 2:23-26 help you maintain a godly perspective when you deal with difficult people?

The Small Stuff

Can any one of you by worrying add a single
hour to your life?
Matthew 6:27

*W*e hear the adage often: don't sweat the small stuff. But as any mom can attest, when we're in the middle of wedding-day bedlam, nothing seems small or insignificant.

After I was escorted to my seat for my daughters' weddings, my brain went into overdrive. Wait, how can I be sitting down? Will the director really know what to do? Shouldn't I be back there? What if my daughter's dress isn't arranged just right? What if her veil is tangled? Why in the world am I sitting here?

Sure enough, when our firstborn floated down the aisle, her cathedral-length veil was curled and twisted. During the opening prayer, I debated whether I should fix it while no one was looking.

No, I reasoned. Let it go. Don't worry about it.

Pause.

I really should step out and straighten the veil.

Fortunately, the pastor stopped praying before I made a decision.

As my friend Kay and her husband approached the front of the church to light the unity candle for their daughter's wedding, she noticed the communion-to-go packets hadn't been opened. Seated in her designated spot, she remained fixated on those packets. We forgot to open the containers, she thought. What if a nervous bride and groom can't open the containers? Why didn't I think of that before? I can't believe we didn't open the communion packets.

Another mom stressed over what guests would think about the length and style of the bridesmaids' dresses. They are too revealing, she thought. I knew they would be. Why didn't I make the girls wear shawls?

Like a thief, wedding-day worries creep in and threaten to snatch away our peace of mind. So many details vie for our attention. Surely, the whole day will fall apart if we don't have our finger on the pulse of every single aspect of it.

Jesus had quite a bit to say about our tendency to worry. "Therefore I tell you, do not worry about your daughter's wedding day, about the communion packets or about the reception food or about your daughter's wedding veil, whether it will be twisted or perfectly arranged."

Actually, that was my paraphrase. Here are the verses as they appear in Scripture:

> Jesus said, "Therefore I tell you, do not worry about your life, what you will eat or drink; or about your body, what you will wear. Is not life more than food, and the body more than clothes? Look at the birds of the air; they do not sow or reap or store away in barns, and yet your heavenly Father feeds them. Are you not much more valuable than they? Can any one of you by worrying add a single hour to your life? And why do you worry about clothes? See how the flowers of the field grow. They do not labor or spin. Yet I tell you that not even Solomon in all his splendor was dressed like one of these" (Matthew 6:25-29).

Our Lord is talking about how we approach each day of our lives, how we respond to the stress of life in the trenches. But could His words be any more relevant to our mother-of-the-bride journey? There is freedom in knowing that our daughter's future doesn't depend on our responses to a thousand decisions.

Listen. Can you hear His voice?

"My dear mother of the bride, don't worry or fret. You belong to Me. Take joy in these moments."

Father, thank You for Your peace-filled words. Help me to remember that You are in full control of this special day and of our family's future. Please give me strength to let go of my worries and to focus on You. May this day bring You honor and glory.

Moment of Grace

Make a list of your wedding worries. Reflect on Matthew 6:25-29 and ask God for the strength and perspective to release those worries to Him.

Come, Let Us Worship

Let us rejoice and be glad and give him glory!
For the wedding of the Lamb has come and his
bride has made herself ready.
Revelation 19:7

The culmination of my sister Charlene's induction into the mother-of-the-bride sisterhood drizzled in on a cool, rainy day just three days after Christmas.

Three days.

After Christmas.

Her world was a head-spinning, ho-ho-ho, here-comes-the-bride, Lord-please-take-me-now, shimmering ball of adventure.

Charlene arrived early to the wedding venue where she helped to arrange seating, oversee table displays, and coordinate with the wedding party. As the hours ticked by, she was the epitome of a multitasker. She supplied hairspray, bobby pins, and garment tape. She answered questions and stocked rooms with enough fast food to sustain the wedding party for days.

My sister didn't stop moving until she came to a door, slightly ajar. She assumed someone behind that door needed her, but when she nudged it open, she saw three of her loved ones with hands clasped and heads bowed in prayer.

The moment grabbed her, and for a few moments, she rested in the eye of the wedding activity storm. Around her, the organized mayhem continued. Bridesmaids searched for safety pins; the caterer rattled dishes and serving trays; questions, giggles, and a dozen conversations buzzed in the adjoining rooms.

But in that one room, our brother-minister, the groom, and the bride "sat" at the feet of Jesus to seek His guidance, favor, and love. They stood on holy ground and worshiped their God.

Remember the story of Mary and Martha recorded in Luke's gospel?

As Jesus and his disciples were on their way, he came to a village where a woman named Martha opened her home to him. She had a sister called Mary, who sat at the Lord's feet listening to what he said. But Martha was distracted by all the preparations that had to be made. She came to him and asked, "Lord, don't you care that my sister has left me to do the work by myself? Tell her to help me!"

"Martha, Martha," the Lord answered, "You are worried and upset about many things, but few things are needed—or indeed only one. Mary has chosen what is better, and it will not be taken away from her." (Luke 10:38-42)

The Lord showed my overworked sister that in her Martha-pace she had almost missed the Mary-experience of basking in the presence of her Creator.

The moment was a reminder that a wedding is about more than a thousand tiny details. It's about worship. It's a day to show reverence and adoration for the One who drew two people into a covenant relationship with each other and with their Creator.

Father, thank You for slowing my frantic pace and for reminding me to be still and to draw close to You. Help me to be intentional about sitting at Your feet. May my heart be so in tune with Yours that I keep Your stillness even as turmoil swirls around me. I love You, Jesus.

Moment of Grace

Take a few minutes to rest in the presence of your Creator. Recite or read Psalm 46:10 several times. In your stillness, thank the Lord for His guidance on this wedding journey and His work in your life.

All about You

I have been crucified with Christ and I no longer live,
but Christ lives in me. The life I now live in the body,
I live by faith in the Son of God, who loved me and
gave himself for me.
Galatians 2:20

Kathy wasn't surprised when her daughter's wedding party sat on the front pew of the church in the middle of the ceremony. Throughout the planning, her daughter and future son-in-law expressed a desire for their wedding day to be a witness to God's work in their lives. They decided that the attendants would sit during the minister's message.

However, Kathy didn't expect what happened next. It took her breath away. The bride and groom also sat on the pew and turned their attention to the minister and to his message of life and hope. In doing so, they shifted their guests' focus from the bride's glory to the glory of the Lord.

The hearts of this young couple were worship-focused. They chose to step out of the spotlight to shine light on the foundation of their relationship—Jesus Christ.

What a beautiful picture of dying to self so Christ would be made known.

What a humbling message.

In the trenches of everyday life, how often do we step aside and redirect focus to our Lord? Far too often we're consumed with ourselves: I'm tired, I'm stressed, I'm overworked. Our world becomes so small that we trample underfoot the thoughts and concerns of others, and we lose the ability to see people through Jesus' eyes. How can we shine light on the Creator of Light if we are focused inward?

The Pharisees in Jesus' day had a focus problem, as illustrated in this story from Luke 18:10-14:

> *Jesus told this parable: "Two men went up to the temple to pray, one a Pharisee and the other a tax collector. The Pharisee stood by himself and prayed: 'God, I thank you that I am not like other people—robbers, evildoers, adulterers—or even like this tax collector. I fast twice a week and give a tenth of all I get.'*

> *"But the tax collector stood at a distance. He would not even look up to heaven, but beat his breast and said, 'God, have mercy on me, a sinner.'*

> *"I tell you that this man, rather than the other, went home justified before God. For all those who exalt themselves will be humbled, and those who humble themselves will be exalted."*

When we read this passage, our instinct may be to bring a hand to our mouths in disgust. How could this holy man be so full of himself? All he does is brag about his goodness.

Then the conviction of the Holy Spirit begins to churn in our hearts.

Yes, He seems to say to us. I see your efforts. You've worked, organized, and sacrificed. You've given much in time and effort. But in all of your busyness and frantic pace, has your focus been on Me? How can others see Me if your plans and actions point to you?

Describing a wedding day as busy is an understatement. We must attend to a multitude of details. But if we forget our purpose for coming together—the covenant of a man and a woman with their heavenly Father—genuine worship can be lost.

May we exhibit the humility of the tax collector and pray, *"God, be merciful to me, a sinner."* Witnessing God's glory in the covenant of marriage is something we don't want to miss.

> *Father God, may my heart sing Your praises, and may my focus be on Your name and Your glory. I repent of my self-absorbed mind-set and ask that You fill me with Your presence. Lord, I love You, and I'm excited about what You are going to do in the lives of Your children.*

Moment of Grace

Read and reflect on Colossians 3:2 and Matthew 6:33. Ask God to reveal areas where you may be absorbing glory meant for Him.

Direct Assault

For our struggle is not against flesh and blood, but against the rulers, against the authorities, against the powers of this dark world and against the spiritual forces of evil in the heavenly realms.
Ephesians 6:12

The big day dawned, not with mild temperatures and gentle breezes, but with air so heavy with heat and humidity that the windows were opaque with a foggy glaze. The bride had slept in curlers to achieve a wavy crown of locks, but because of the weather, her efforts were futile.

Then the rain began—huge, driving drops that drenched the celebratory spirits of the bewildered wedding party.

Arriving at the wedding venue, the mother of the bride encountered a few cold shoulders instead of welcoming arms. Extended family complained that children hadn't been invited to the event. One person refused even to speak to the mother of the bride but made sure that everyone else heard about her displeasure.

As the bride dressed, a bridesmaid inadvertently placed a streak of mascara across the front of the bridal gown.

Then word arrived about an accident on a major highway into town. Several guests came too late to witness the ceremony. No one lit the candles in the reception hall, which spoiled all the hard work and preparation intended to create the right ambiance.

The dazed mom spent the first part of the reception searching for trash receptacles. She muttered, "Why am I running around looking for trash cans? I'm the mother of the bride."

At the end of the day, no one stayed to help the bride's family clean the venue.

The exhausted mother's spirits mirrored the weather conditions. Her thoughts tumbled and swirled as she struggled to concentrate on her lengthy cleanup list. The whispery voices in her head were clear and mocking: what a disaster.

And that's how he works—you know, God's adversary, Satan.

He reaches his grimy claws into our circumstances, attacks our hearts, and shreds our fragile peace. Under assault, we're tempted to cower, for surely our present state of affairs bears witness to his victory.

But if we listen to another voice—one infinitely more loving, wise, and dear—we'll hear truth. And that truth will soothe our bruised souls.

Thank you for your worship.

We're stunned. "Worship? Lord, have You been paying attention? Nothing went according to plan."

In the vows given today, I was honored and glorified. I was here, in this place, as my children entered into a covenant relationship with Me.

And that's how He works—you know, our Creator, Redeemer, Savior. With gentle loving-kindness, He reaches into our circumstances, not to mock us but to show us how He continues to work His plans and purposes in and through us.

Even when we can't see or understand.

Even when it seems we are neck-deep in disaster and failure.

As the beleaguered mom entered into wedding-recovery mode, God healed her heart with His Word and through the encouragement of wedding guests. Many said the ceremony had been a testimony to them, and they had experienced worship.

Even in the unexpected, God reached into the lives of the wedding party and glorified Himself through them.

Yes, that's how He works.

Lord God, I stand in awe of You. To know that You're always at work fulfilling Your purposes gives me such joy. Help me to find rest and peace in Your sovereignty. Even when I can't see what You're doing, give me strength to trust Your heart. Thank You, Jesus.

Moment of Grace

Take time to marvel at how God works in the midst of stressful circumstances. Write a praise note to Him, thanking Him for several specific ways you've seen His sovereignty at work in this wedding journey.

In Recovery

But those who hope in the Lord will renew their strength.
They will soar on wings like eagles; they will run and not
grow weary, they will walk and not be faint.

Isaiah 40:31

At 2:00 a.m. on the morning after Laura's wedding, Roy and I sat on the couch at home and started to eat our first piece of her wedding cake.

I still wore my blue-green dream dress, minus the jacket. Heels and hose had been replaced with flip-flops, and my jewelry lay in a small heap on the coffee table. My sweetheart reclined with tie askew and shirttail untucked, his plate of cake balanced on his lap.

Neither of us spoke.

In the next room, our two younger daughters slept, exhausted from hours of celebration. It wasn't the first time one of our children's beds was empty. Our family had been in transition for a while. But that night was different. The house seemed different—bigger, emptier. The marriage line had been crossed, and some things would never be the same.

We had no time to process it, however, because Mary, our middle daughter, was leaving for her summer job that morning. We had to be at the airport, which was an hour's drive away, by 9:00 a.m.

Mary would be away from home for the entire summer, something she'd never experienced. God had called her to be a camp counselor and work with young children. She'd be traveling to several camps in a variety of states over the next couple of months. The airport good-byes were difficult, but she was confident in following God's plan.

We had just walked through a huge emotional send-off for her big sister, so we were all weepy and exhausted. My heart tightened at the vulnerability in Mary's eyes. I thought about the incredible impact this job would have on her life, even without the emotional storm of a family wedding. With tears and prayers, our family huddled for one more good-bye.

One more temporary separation.

One more letting go.

Back in the airport parking lot, my husband, our youngest daughter, Katie, and I were quiet for several minutes before I managed to squeak out, "So this mama is hungry. How about you guys?"

We drove to the South's solution for stress-reduction—Cracker Barrel Old Country Store and Restaurant. An hour with good ole country cookin' was what our weary souls needed. We waited for our table to be ready and tried to relax by sharing hugs, smiles, and snippets of memories from the wedding.

The fatigue in those moments was intense, but everything would be okay. Together we'd adjust to this new season of life. Katie even made a joke or two about the perks of being an only child and receiving our undivided attention.

Then the restaurant host led us to a table and seated us beside a young family. And there, two feet away, right beside my chair, was a sleeping infant in a baby carrier. If the Cracker Barrel Old Country Store and Restaurant folks trained their employees in accordance with mother-of-the-bride guidelines, this never would have happened. I glared at the young man who had seated us.

My interior dialogue with him went something like this: Are you kidding me? Do you have any idea what I've been through the past twenty-four hours, not to mention the last ten months? Why, oh why, would you seat me beside a baby? Do you not know? Have you not heard? I waved good-bye to two of my children in the past few hours. Two. Of my children. I mean, seriously. Yesterday, they were babies. Today, they're on airplanes— without their mother. Do you hear me, you young, clueless whippersnapper? And no, I don't want sweet tea. It's 9:30 in the morning, for crying out loud.

It was probably the first time I had ever used the word *whippersnapper*, and thankfully, my rant stayed within the confines of my stressed-out brain. I put my back to the baby and made it through the meal without further incident.

We laugh about it now, but that morning at the restaurant was the beginning of my wedding recovery. We had talked, planned, and prepared for the coming changes to our family, but the actual transition took major adjustments. Staying in God's Word, holding on to His promises of peace and strength, was crucial for me. I clung to verses such as Psalm 29:11—*The Lord gives strength to his people; the Lord blesses his people with peace.* I clutched Isaiah 26:3—*You will keep in perfect peace him whose mind is steadfast, because he trusts in you.*

I felt these life changes spiritually, physically, and emotionally. I needed my Lord's help to take the next steps. Thankfully, He supported me with His everlasting strength and love and held my hand as I stumbled alongside Him.

Oh, Father, how I praise You for Your faithfulness! When You walked this earth, You experienced the same sadness and loneliness I'm feeling. You know, and You understand. Help me to remember that You'll never leave me or forsake me. Even when it seems the ground is shifting beneath me, You are forever faithful and true. I love You, Jesus.

Moment of Grace

Soak in the beautiful, comforting words of Colossians 3:15. When emotions threaten to overwhelm you, how can you let the peace of Christ rule in your heart?

The Connection

Know therefore that the Lord your God is God; he is the faithful God, keeping his covenant of love to a thousand generations of those who love him and keep his commandments.

Deuteronomy 7:9

Kay took a breath and stared at the object in her hand—her daughter's cell phone. Someone discovered it in the mounds of wedding-day debris, and the exhausted mom now held it with a vice-like grip.

Remnants of conversations bounced around in her muddled brain. According to witnesses, the wedding had been beautiful, a cherished time of praise and worship for the gathered family and friends. An abundance of food and fellowship made the reception a success. The newlyweds had departed for their wedding trip, and most of the guests had left as well.

It was time to tackle the cleanup.

But Kay was frozen in place, her gaze fixed on the cell phone. Panic spread its turbulence from her mind to her heart. This is my daughter's phone. She doesn't have her phone. How will she contact me? What if she needs me? I don't know how to fix this.

Her daughter's new mother-in-law stepped up and offered to take the phone to the couple's apartment, but Kay couldn't release it. Yes, she thought. I should give her the phone. That will work. Give her the phone.

No. This is my little girl's phone. I can't let it go.

Logic slipped away like a fading mist, and the overtired mom tightened her hold on what felt like the last connection to her daughter. It didn't occur to her that, if necessary, the bride could use her new husband's phone. All that mattered was that this phone, this connection, was severed. Broken. Unusable.

A wave of loss swept over her, and its force nearly drove her to her knees. She's married. She's really married.

Kay experienced what so many of us do in our daughter's wedding journey—an overwhelming sense of loss. From our child's first day of kindergarten, separation is a continuous process: let go, let go, let go. We assume that all the minor letting-goes will prepare us for the major ones, such as marriage. But we're still stunned, unbalanced by the rush of emotions we feel.

Lord, what just happened?

In the days and weeks of transition, our dependence on our heavenly Father is our lifeline. He is faithful to us and to our children. He loves and cares for our children more than we could dream or imagine, and He holds their future (and ours) in the palm of His hand. *"For I know the plans I have for you," declares the Lord, "plans to prosper you and not to harm you, plans to give you hope and a future"* (Jeremiah 29:11).

We have poured our heart and soul into our daughters, but now our role changes. We're no longer responsible for their physical well-being, but our concern for them never diminishes.

And guess what? We never stop praying for them. We can always seek the Lord's heart for our daughters. We can ask Him to give them the strength and courage to be all He designed them to be. We can remain open and available when they ask for our input and advice. We can take joy in their journey.

Our connection with our daughters may look different, but it's still there—solid, fresh, and brimming with possibilities. A grown-up adventure awaits us, one we can explore together. With the strength of our Lord, we can step out in faith and embrace this relationship and the plans He has for us and our daughters.

Father God, I praise You for the honor and privilege of being a mother. Watching my daughter grow into a young woman with plans and dreams of her own has been an adventure and a gift. Guide me as I transition into this new relationship. May I seek Your heart on my daughter's behalf and know that You alone hold her future. I trust You, Jesus.

Moment of Grace

Read Lamentations 3:22-26. Make a list of ways God has shown His faithfulness to your daughter. Praise Him for His unchanging love.

Melancholy Baby

Truly he is my rock and my salvation; he is my fortress,
I will not be shaken.
Psalms 62:6

"*I* felt so blue. I was happy. I am happy. I don't know. The whole experience has been good and joyful and everything. It's just that ..."

As my friend Mary struggled to express her post-wedding emotions, she sighed. In that sigh swirled a lifetime of mother-memories. Memories of a girl, a young woman, and a glowing bride. Even though her daughter's growth spanned years, it seemed as if it happened in moments.

My heart went out to my friend. I understood her turmoil. On some days I thought I had moved on, then a memory would ambush me—the girls outside on the swing set or sitting at the kitchen counter, legs swinging from a barstool. As moms, we may feel off balance as we struggle to find solid footing in this new life season. But let's call it what it is—grief. We're releasing the used-to-be and turning to grasp at the unknown.

And I've noticed something. Daddies also grieve, but they grieve in a more efficient manner. My husband was quiet in the days before the weddings. He was letting go of his girls. Then a day or two after each event, he looked ahead to the next challenge. He was ready to conquer new worlds.

But while he was conquering, I was saying, "Hey, wait! I'm not ready for this."

The Lord understands our struggle with transition. His Word is packed with stories of people walking through transition and change. The common thread? Change is vital to growth. Think about it. When we accept God's gift of salvation, we turn (change) from our sinful behavior and reach for purity and holiness. In our Christ-walk, the Holy Spirit works in our lives to move (transition) us into deeper fellowship. *Do not conform to the pattern of this world, but be transformed by the renewing of your mind. Then you will be able to test and approve what God's will is—his good, pleasing and perfect will* (Romans 12:2).

But here's the exciting part. While God desires growth and transformation in us, changes that make us more like Him, He doesn't change. *The Lord is my rock, my fortress and my deliverer; my God is my rock, in whom I take refuge, my shield and the horn of my salvation, my stronghold* (Psalm 18:2).

Rock. Fortress. Deliverer.

How comforting.

How beautiful.

When our heart cries out for stability, when we feel flooded with the grief of letting go, our Lord is there, waiting to embrace us with arms of loving-kindness.

Father, I'm thankful for Your steady hand over these last months. But sometimes the grief rushes in and steals my breath. When this happens, help me to turn to You, my refuge and my shield. Infuse me with Your strength and give me courage to walk through this transition. Lord, may I glorify You with my life.

Moment of Grace

Read and meditate on Proverbs 18:10 and Exodus 15:2. How do these verses strengthen and comfort you?

Reflection and Praise

Praise the Lord. Praise God in his sanctuary; praise him in his mighty heavens. Praise him for his acts of power; praise him for his surpassing greatness. Praise him with the sounding of the trumpet, praise him with the harp and lyre, praise him with timbrel and dancing, praise him with the strings and pipe, praise him with the clash of cymbals, praise him with resounding cymbals. Let everything that has breath praise the Lord. Praise the Lord.
Psalm 150

I lean against the doorframe of the room where she used to sleep. My gaze moves over stuffed animals, sports trophies, and an old pair of sneakers. Photos and posters dot the walls, evidence of former priorities. Red basketball shorts peek from a half-closed drawer.

I linger, letting my mind drift over the years. I allow myself to remember the toddler, the teen, and the young woman. And for the moment, I feel no sadness. With my whole heart, I want to lift my voice in praise.

The Creator of the Universe lovingly formed a child and placed her in my care. For more than eighteen years, she was "mine." God gave me the privilege of nurturing her, guiding her in His ways. He gifted me with moments known only to Him and me—treasured eternal instants when I was a part of my daughter's life, when I watched, touched, loved, and held her.

My heart swells with praise for God's forgiveness, patience, and longsuffering. This flawed mom made a zillion mistakes. I'm overcome with gratitude to my redeemer, because in my weakness, He is made strong. His words from 2 Corinthians 12:9 settle in my heart and mind: *My grace is sufficient for you, for my power is made perfect in weakness.*

Alone in the house, I lift my hands and my voice. "Yes, Lord. Your grace is sufficient. You honored my feeble efforts. Thank You. Thank You." As my heart praises Him, I worship. *Come, let us bow down in worship, let us kneel before the Lord our Maker* (Psalm 95:6). *Sing to the Lord, for he has done glorious things; let this be known to all the world* (Isaiah 12:5). Yes, my Lord has done glorious things. Joy fills my heart as I bask in His presence.

Once again, life is in transition. The path ahead rounds a corner. I can't see what lies beyond. But I know the One who waits for me. He stands ready, loving me and encouraging me to take those steps of faith into the grand adventure of His plans and purposes.

I inhale deeply and place my hand in His.

I'm ready, Lord. Let's do this.

I will exalt you, my God the King; I will praise your name for ever and ever. Every day I will praise you and extol your name for ever and ever. Great is the Lord and most worthy of praise; his greatness no one can fathom. One generation commends your works to another; they tell of your mighty acts. They speak of the glorious splendor of your majesty—and I will meditate on your wonderful works. They tell of the power of your awesome works—and I will proclaim your great deeds. They celebrate your abundant goodness and joyfully sing of your righteousness. (Psalm 145:1-7)

Moment of Grace

Meditate on the wonderful works of the Lord in your life and ask for His guidance in this time of transition. Write a letter of thanksgiving and praise to God for the gift of walking with your daughter through this wedding journey.